D1744123

THE LAMENTATIONS OF JEREMIAH

A BRIEF EXPOSITION

by

William Kelly

CHAPTER TWO
LONDON • ENGLAND

THE LAMENTATIONS OF JEREMIAH

by

William Kelly

ISBN 1 85307 149 8

First published in 1871 in the *Bible Treasury* Vol. 8, p. 200 etc. [in 7 parts]. Here with a prologue from *God's Inspiration of the Scriptures* by W.K. 1903

Published in Russian 1992 by GBV Dillenburg, Germany
This edition published 1999

DISTRIBUTORS

- Bible, Book and Tract Depôt, 23 Santarosa Avenue, Ryde, NSW 2112, Australia
- Bible House, Gateway Mall, 35 Tudor Street, Bridgetown, Barbados, WI
- Believers Bookshelf, 5205 Regional Road 81, Unit 3, Beamsville, ON, L0R 1B3, Canada
- Bible Treasury Bookstore, 46 Queen Street, Dartmouth, Nova Scotia, B2Y 1G1, Canada
- Bibles & Publications Chrétiennes, 30 rue Châteauvert, 26000 Valence, France
- CSV, An der Schloßfabrik 30, 42499 Hückeswagen, Germany
- Christian Truth Bookroom, Paddisonpet, Tenali 522 201, Andhra Pradesh, India
- Words of Life Trust, 3 Chuim, Khar, Mumbai, 400 052, India
- Uit het Woord der Waarheid, Postbox 260, 7120AG Aalten, Netherlands
- Bible and Book Depot, Box 25119, Christchurch 5, New Zealand
- Kristen Litteratur, Tjøsvoll øst, 4270 Åkrehamn, Norway
- Grace & Truth Book-room, 87 Chaussee Road, Castries, St. Lucia, WI
- Beröa Verlag, Zellerstrasse 61, 8038 Zürich, Switzerland
- Dépôt de Bibles et Traités Chrétiens, 4 rue du Nord, 1800 Vevey, Switzerland
- Chapter Two Bookshop, 199 Plumstead Common Road, London, SE18 2UJ, UK
- HoldFast Bible & Tract Depôt, 100 Camden Road, Tunbridge Wells, Kent, TN1 2QP, UK
- Words of Truth, PO Box 147, Belfast, BT8 4TT, Northern Ireland, UK
- Believers Bookshelf Inc., Box 261, Sunbury, PA 17801, USA

edited and typeset at Chapter Two
printed in Germany by BasseDruck, 58121 Hagen

PROLOGUE

THE last chapter 52 of Jeremiah is expressly an appendix to the words of Jeremiah by the inspired editor. It is a most appropriate close of the prophecy and introduction to the Lamentations.

It is notable, but by no means an unprecedented thing, that the book, which more than any other breathes the distress of a pious and broken heart, is clothed in a markedly artificial form. God meant His people to share the prophet's lamentation; and its predominant shape occupied his heart who wrote, and theirs who pondered and remembered it all the more. Its five chapters are five elegies. Chapters 1 and 2 have twenty-two stanzas or verses, answering to the letters of the Hebrew alphabet, and each stanza with three parts. In the third chapter the initial letter occurs for each of the three parts, when the prophet speaks personally of his own sufferings, as before and after chapter 3 he pours forth his groans over the city destroyed with all its glories. In chapter 4 each stanza consists of two parts, each verse beginning with the successive letters of the alphabet. Though chapter 5 has twenty-two stanzas or verses of two parts, the initial letters do not follow regularly. It is throughout a true-hearted confession of sins. "The crown is fallen from our head; woe unto us for we have sinned! For this our heart is faint; for these things our eyes have grown dim, because of the mountain of Zion, which is desolate: foxes walk over it. Thou, Jehovah, dwellest for ever; thy throne is from generation to generation. Wherefore dost thou forget us for ever—dost thou forsake us so long time? Turn thou us unto thee, Jehovah, and we shall be turned; renew our days as of old. Or is it that thou hast utterly rejected us—art wroth with us exceedingly?"

The book has then a place quite unique, from a heart which answered to the love of Jehovah for His people, when they were most justly in the depths because of their sins and His chastisement, even to blotting them out from His land, city, kingdom, and house. It is thorough self-judgment in the heart's solidarity with them and clinging in the face and experience of all to Him. Can we not discern what a gap for the Bible if we had not Lamentations? What will it not be to the godly in their last tribulation? Did the writer forget his own purchase (Jer. 32.) in faith of the word? or his prophecy of Israel under Messiah and the new covenant? Assuredly not; yet none the less did he mourn the ruin of Israel, and that Jehovah should have grounds so valid for His severe chastening.

from *God's Inspiration of the Scriptures* by WK

INTRODUCTION

IT IS no uncommon thought now, as of old, to
assume that the book on which we are now entering
consists of the Lamentations written by the prophet
on the occasion of Josiah's death. (2 Chron. 35:25).
If a divine testimony affirmed this, it would be our
place to believe it: to that no one pretends, still there
is the secret assumption that what Jeremiah composed
in sorrow for Josiah must be in the Bible, and hence
must be this book. But there is no sufficient reason to
conclude that all the writings of prophets were
inspired for the permanent use of God's people: rather
is there good ground to conclude that they were not.
Hence we are free to examine the character of the
work before us, not to question its divine authority
but to ascertain as far as may be its aim and the
subjects of which it treats. But, if so, the contents
themselves are adverse to the idea; for the distressing
prostration of Jerusalem, not the death of the pious
king cut down so young, is clearly in view. The
description of the state of the city, sanctuary, and
people does not accord with Josiah's death; and even
the king, whose humiliation is named (Lam. 2:9),
could not possibly be Josiah, who was slain in battle,
instead of being among the Gentiles and therefore in
captivity. It was no doubt Jehoiachin whose varied
lot we can easily trace by comparing the prophecy

and 2 Kings 24, 25. All the circumstances of that time tally with the bewailings here.

That the Spirit of prophecy dictated the book cannot be justly doubted, though it may not have direct predictions like the former work from which in the Hebrew Bible it has long been severed as to place, though not so in the days of Josephus. Nevertheless the distinctness of object, tone, and manner is sufficiently marked to justify our viewing it as a separate work of the same writer, Jeremiah. It was morally good that we should have not only predictions of the deep trouble coming on the house of David and Jerusalem, but also the outpouring of a godly heart broken by anguish for the people of God, and the more because they deserved all that fell upon them through their enemies at God's hand. We little think what such an one as Jeremiah must have felt to see the temple destroyed, the holy service suspended, the king and priests and bulk of Judah carried off by their idolatrous conqueror, compelled to own also that their desolation was most righteous because of their sins. Even when he had survived the events which proved the value of his own slighted prophecies, he was inspired to pour forth these elegies which were no vain complaints as we shall see, but a spreading out of the woes of the city and people before a God whose compassion and faithfulness are alike infinite. He vindicates God in what He had done to unhappy Jerusalem. He places before God the utter ruin of the people, civilly and religiously, charging the false prophets with luring them into the pit by their falsehood and flattery, but exhorting the people to repentance. He shows his own sense of sorrow

deeper than that of any other, as indeed he both
suffered peculiarly from the Jews themselves before
the crash came, and the Spirit of Christ that was in
him gave him to realize all, where others nerved
themselves to brave it with the mailed armour of
insensibility and indomitable pride; yet does he
cherish hope in what God is, who loves to lift up the
fallen and abase the proud. He contrasts their present
misery, because of the sins of their priests and
prophets, with their former prosperity, but declares
that an end will be to Zion's punishment, but none to
Edom's. Lastly, he prayerfully spreads out all their
own calamities before Jehovah; his only confidence
too is in Him who can turn us to Himself, whatever
may be His just wrath.

The form is very notable; save in the last chapter,
all are acrostic or at least alphabetic. De Wette, with
the usual arrogance of a rationalist, pronounces this of
itself as an offspring of the later vitiated taste. But
this he must do in defiance of the plain fact that those
admirable and even early Psalms 25, 34, 37 are
similarly constructed, not to speak of the wonderful
Psalm 119 and several others in the same fifth book
of the Psalter (111, 112, 145). Those who pronounce
these psalms cold, feeble, and flat, as well as
unconnected, simply betray their own lack of all just
appreciation, not to speak of reverence which we may
not expect from men who deny them in any true sense
to be of God. The first, second, and fourth chapters
are so written that each verse begins with one of the
twenty-two letters of the Hebrew alphabet in due
succession, save that in the second and fourth ע
follows instead of preceding פ; and the same

transposition occurs in Lam. 3, where we have three verses instead of single ones, which so commence; and hence there are in it 66 verses.   Another peculiarity is to be noticed, that each verse (except Lam. 1:7, Lam. 2:19) is a sort of triplet in chapters 1, 2, 3. Lam. 4 is characterized by couplets (save ver. 15); and a singular structure is traceable in Lam. 5, save that it does not begin with the letters of the alphabet, though it consists of twenty-two verses. 'Difference of authorship" is the ready but monotonous cry of dark scepticism: others as despairing of intelligence impute it to *forgetfulness*, a third to *accident!* The propriety of the change in what throughout is a prayer and confession to Jehovah must be apparent to the spiritual mind.   The alphabetic form may have had a mnemonic object in view. For pathos the book as a whole is unequalled.

LAMENTATIONS 1

THE prophet presents a graphic view of Jerusalem once abounding with people now sitting alone, and as a widow; she that was mighty among nations, a princess among the provinces, now become tributary. She is seen weeping sore, and this in the night when darkness and sleep bring respite to others, to her only a renewal of that grief, less restrained, which covers her cheeks with tears. Now is proved the folly as well as the sin that forsook Jehovah for others; but there is for her no comforter out of her lovers. All her friends, the allies she counted on, deal treacherously by her, and are but enemies. (ver. 1, 2).

The last hope of the nation was gone. Israel had been long a prey to the Assyrian. But now in the captivity of Judah mourning overspreads Zion where once were crowded feasts. And there is no exception to the rule of affliction: her priests sigh, her virgins are afflicted, herself as a whole in bitterness. On the other hand her adversaries are in power and command over her. How bitter was all this to a Jew! and in a sense most bitter where the Jew was godly. For besides the grief of nature he might share with his countrymen, there was the added and poignant sorrow that the normal witnesses of Jehovah on earth had proved false, and he could not see how glory would be brought to God in spite of and through Israel's unfaithfulness.

It is necessary to bear in mind the peculiar place of Israel and Jerusalem: otherwise we can never appreciate such a book as this, and many of the Psalms, as well as much of the Prophets. The patriotism of a Jew was bound up as that of no other people or country was with the honour of Jehovah. Providence governs everywhere: no raid of Red Indians, no manoeuvre of the greatest military power in the West, no movement or struggle in Asia, without His eye and hand. But He had set up a direct government in His own land and people, modified from Samuel's days by kingly power, which had blessing guaranteed on obedience. But who could guarantee the obedience? Israel pledged it indeed, but in vain. The people disobeyed, the priests disobeyed, the kings disobeyed. We see too that in Jeremiah's days false prophets imitated the true, and supplanted them in the heed of a court and nation which desired a delusive sanction from God on their own wilfulness, prophesying what pleased the people in flattery and deceit. Hence the corruption only lent an immense impetus to those who were already hastening down the steep of ruin. But this did not lesson the agony of such as Jeremiah. They realized the inevitable ruin; and he, not in moral sense only but by divine inspiration, gives expression to his feelings here. The blessed Lord Jesus Himself is the perfect pattern of similar grief over Jerusalem, in Him absolutely unselfish and in every way pure, but so much the more deeply felt. Unless the relation of that city to God be understood, one cannot enter into this; and there is danger of either explaining it away into care for their souls, or of perverting it into a ground for

similar feelings, each for his own country. But it is
clear that a man's soul is the same in Pekin or
London, in Jerusalem or Baltimore. The Lord does
show us the immeasurable value of a soul elsewhere;
but this is not the key to His tears over Jerusalem.
The impending judgment of God in this world, the
dismal consequences yet in the womb of the future,
because of the rejection of the Messiah as well as all
other evil against God, made the Saviour weep. We
cannot wonder therefore that the Spirit of Christ
which was in Jeremiah, and guided him in this Book
of Lamentations, gave the prophet communion with
his Master before He Himself proved its worst against
His own person.

God might raise up a fresh testimony, as we know
He has done; but, while bowing to His sovereign will,
the utter ruin of the old witness justly filled the heart
of every pious God-fearing Israelite with sorrow
unceasing; and surely not the less "because Jehovah
hath afflicted her for the multitude of her
transgressions." Grief is not less over God's people
because they have dishonoured God and are
righteously chastised. "Her children are gone into
captivity before the enemy. And from the daughter of
Zion all her beauty is departed: her princes are as
harts which find no pasture and go powerless before
the pursuer."

There was the bitter aggravation, ever present, of
what the city of the great King had lost, which He,
when He came and was refused, told out in His
broken words of weeping over it. "Jerusalem
remembered in the days of her affliction and of her
miseries all her pleasant things that she had in the

days of old, when her people fell into the hand of the enemy, and none did help her: the adversaries saw her, and did mock at her sabbaths. Jerusalem hath grievously sinned; therefore she is removed: all that honoured her despise her, because they have seen her nakedness: yea, she sigheth, and turneth backward. Her filthiness is in her skirts; she remembereth not her last end; therefore she came down wonderfully: she had no comforter. O Jehovah, behold my affliction: for the enemy hath magnified himself. The adversary hath spread out his hand upon all her pleasant things: for she hath seen that the heathen entered into her sanctuary, whom thou didst command that they should not enter into thy congregation. All her people sigh, they seek bread; they have given their pleasant things for meat to relieve the soul: see, O Jehovah, and consider: for I am become vile." (ver. 7-11). Faith however sees in the prostration of the guilty city under the relentless adversary a plea for Jehovah's compassion and interposition on its behalf.

Then the prophet personifies the downtrodden Zion turning to the passing strangers for their pity. "Is it nothing to you, all ye that pass by? behold, and see if there be any sorrow like unto my sorrow, which is done unto me, wherewith Jehovah hath afflicted me in the day of his fierce anger. From above hath he sent fire into my bones, and it prevaileth against them: he hath spread a net for my feet, he hath turned me back: he hath made me desolate and faint all the day. The yoke of my transgressions is bound by his hand: they are wreathed, and come up upon my neck: he hath made my strength to fall, the Lord hath delivered me into their hands, from whom I am not able to rise up. The Lord hath trodden under foot all my mighty men in the midst of me: he hath called an assembly against me to crush my young men: the Lord hath trodden the virgin, the daughter of Judah, as in a winepress. For these things I weep; mine eye, mine eye runneth down with water, because the comforter that should relieve my soul is far from me: my children are desolate, because the enemy prevailed." (ver. 12-16). Still all is traced to Jehovah's dealing because of Jerusalem's rebellious sins; and hence He is morally vindicated. "Zion spreadeth forth her hands, and there is none to comfort her: Jehovah hath commanded concerning Jacob, that his adversaries should be round about him: Jerusalem is as a menstruous woman among them. Jehovah is righteous; for I have rebelled against his commandment: hear, I pray you, all people, and behold my sorrow: my virgins and my young men are gone into captivity. I called for my lovers, but they deceived me: my priests and mine elders gave up the ghost in the city, while they sought their meat to relieve their souls." (ver. 17-19).

Finally, Jehovah is called to behold, because Jerusalem was thus troubled, and this too inwardly, because of its own grievous rebellion; and He is besought to requite the enemy who took pleasure in their abject shame and deep suffering. "Behold, O Jehovah; for I am in distress: my bowels are troubled; mine heart is turned within me; for I have grievously rebelled: abroad the sword bereaveth, at home there is as death. They have heard that I sigh: there is none to comfort me: all mine enemies have heard of my trouble, they are glad that thou hast done it; thou wilt bring the day that thou hast called, and they shall be like unto me. Let all their wickedness come before thee; and do unto them as thou hast done unto me for all my transgressions: for my sighs are many, and my heart is faint." (ver. 20-22).

LAMENTATIONS 2

IT has been noticed that the solitude of Jerusalem is the prominent feeling expressed in the opening of these elegies. Here we shall find its overthrow spread out in the strongest terms and with great detail. Image is crowded on image to express the completeness of the destruction to which Jehovah had devoted His own chosen people, city, and temple; the more terrible, as He must be in His own nature and purpose unchangeable. None felt the truth of His love to Israel more than the prophet; for this very reason, none could so deeply feel the inevitable blows of His hand, obliged as He was to be an enemy to those He most loved. "How hath the Lord covered the daughter of Zion with the cloud in his anger, and cast down from heaven unto the earth the beauty of Israel, and remembered not his footstool in the day of his anger. The Lord hath swallowed up all the habitations of Jacob, and hath not pitied: he hath thrown down in his wrath the strongholds of the daughter of Judah; he hath brought them down to the ground: he hath polluted the kingdom and the princes thereof. He hath cut off in his fierce anger all the horn of Israel: he hath drawn back his right hand from before the enemy, and he burned against Jacob like a flaming fire, which devoureth round about. He hath bent his bow like an enemy: he stood with his right hand as an adversary, and slew all that were pleasant to the eye in the tabernacle of the daughter of Zion: he poured out his fury like fire. The Lord was as an enemy: he hath swallowed up Israel, he hath swallowed up all her palaces: he hath destroyed his strongholds, and hath increased in the daughter of Judah mourning and lamentation." (ver. 1-5).

But even this was not the worst. Their civil degradation and ruin were dreadful; for their outward place and blessings came from God in a sense peculiar to Israel. But what was this to His degrading His own earthly dwelling in their midst! "And he hath violently taken away his tabernacle, as if it were of a garden: he hath destroyed his places of the assembly. Jehovah hath caused the solemn feasts and sabbaths to be forgotten in Zion, and hath despised in the indignation of his anger the king and the priest. The Lord hath cast off his altar, he hath abhorred his sanctuary, he hath given up into the hand of the enemy the walls of her palaces; they have made a noise in the house of Jehovah, as in the day of a solemn feast." (ver. 6, 7). It was of no use to think of the Chaldeans. God it was who brought Zion and the temple, and their feasts and fasts and sacrifices, with king and priest, to nought.

Hence in verse 8 it is said with yet greater emphasis, "Jehovah hath purposed to destroy the wall of the daughter of Zion: he hath stretched out a line, he hath not withdrawn his hand from destroying: therefore he made the rampart and the wall to lament; they languished together. Her gates are sunk into the ground; he hath destroyed and broken her bars: her king and her princes are among the Gentiles: the law is no more; her prophets also find no vision from

Jehovah. The elders of the daughter of Zion sit upon the ground and keep silence: they have cast up dust upon their heads; they have girded themselves with sackcloth: the virgins of Jerusalem hang down their heads to the ground." (ver. 8-10). The prophet then introduces his own grief. "Mine eyes do fill with tears, my bowels are troubled, my liver is poured upon the earth, for the destruction of the daughter of my people; because the children and the sucklings swoon in the streets of the city. They say to their mothers, Where is corn and wine? when they swooned as the wounded in the streets of the city, when their soul was poured out into their mothers' bosom. What thing shall I take to witness for thee? what thing shall I liken to thee, O daughter of Jerusalem? what shall I equal to thee, that I may comfort thee, O virgin daughter of Zion? for thy breach is great like the sea: who can heal thee?" He justly feels that no object can adequately match the miseries of Zion. The sea alone could furnish by its greatness a notion of the magnitude of their calamities.

Another element now enters to aggravate the description—the part which false prophets played before the final crisis came. "Thy prophets have seen vain and foolish things for thee: and they have not discovered thine iniquity, to turn away thy captivity; but have seen for thee false burdens and causes of banishment." (ver. 14).

Then he depicts the cruel satisfaction of their envious neighbours over their sufferings and ruin. "All that pass by clap their hands at thee; they hiss and wag their head at the daughter of Jerusalem, saying, Is this the city that men call the perfection of beauty, the joy of the whole earth? All thine enemies have opened their mouth against thee: they hiss and gnash the teeth: they say, We have swallowed her up: certainly this is the day that we looked for; we have found, we have seen it." (ver. 15, 16) But the prophet insists that it was Jehovah who had done the work of destruction because of His people's iniquity, let the Gentiles boast as they might of their power over Jerusalem. "Jehovah hath done that which he had devised; he hath fulfilled his word that he had commanded in the days of old: he hath thrown down and hath not pitied: and he hath caused thine enemy to rejoice over thee, he hath set up the horn of thine adversaries." (ver. 17).   Sorrowful, most sorrowful, that His hand had done it all; yet a comfort to faith, for it is the hand that can and will build up again for His name's sake. Nor was it a hasty chastening; from earliest days Jehovah had threatened and predicted by Moses what Jeremiah details in his Lamentations. Compare Lev. 26, Deut. 28, 31, 32. To Him therefore the prophet would have the heart to cry really, as it had in vain through mere vexation. "Their heart cried unto the Lord, O wall of the daughter of Zion, let tears run down like a river day and night: give thyself no rest; let not the apple of thine eye cease. Arise, cry out in the night: in the beginning of the watches pour out thine heart like water before the face of the Lord: lift up thy hands toward him for the life of thy young children, that faint for hunger in the top of every street. Behold, O Jehovah, and consider to whom thou hast done this. Shall the women eat their fruit, and children of a span long? shall the priest and the prophet be slain in the sanctuary of the Lord? The young and the old lie on the ground in the streets: my virgins and my young men are fallen by the sword; thou hast slain them in the day of thine anger; thou hast killed, and not pitied. Thou hast called as in a solemn day my terrors round about, so that in the day of Jehovah's anger none escaped nor remained: those that I have swaddled and brought up hath mine enemy consumed." (ver. 18-22). He arrays the most frightful excesses the Jews had suffered before God that He may deal with the enemies who had been thus guilty.

As to the apparent alphabetic dislocation in verses 16, 17, I do not doubt that it is intentional. In Lam. 1 all is regular as to this. In Lam. 3, Lam. 4 a transposition occurs similar to what we find here. It cannot therefore be either accidental on the one hand, or due to a different order in the alphabet on the other, as has been thought. Some of the Hebrew MSS. place the verses as they should stand in the regular order, and the Septuagint pursues a middle course by inverting the alphabetic marks but retaining the verses to which they should belong in their Masoretic place. But there is no sufficient reason to doubt that the Hebrew gives the passage as the Spirit inspired it, spite of the strangeness of the order, which must therefore have been meant to heighten the picture of sorrow. In sense they must stand as they are: a change according to the ordinary place of the initials פ and ע would cut the thread of just connection.

LAMENTATIONS 3:1-21

THIS strain differs, as in the triple alliteration of its structure, so also in its more distinctly personal plaintiveness. The prophet expresses his own sense of sorrow, no longer representing Zion but speaking for himself, while at the same time his grief is bound up with the people, and none the less because he was an object of derision and hatred to them for his love to them in faithfulness to Jehovah. Other prophets may have been exempted for special ends of God, but none tasted the bitterness of Israel's portion more keenly than Jeremiah. His desire is that others should bear the grief of the people's state as here expressed for the heart in order to final comfort and blessing from God. In the opening verses he tells out his experiences in trouble. "I am the man that hath seen affliction by the rod of his wrath." He hath led me and brought me into darkness, but not into light. Surely against me is he turned; he turneth his hand against me all the day." (ver. 1-3). He owns it to be from Jehovah's hand and rod. Indignation was gone forth from God against Israel, and a true-hearted prophet was the last one to screen himself or wish it. There was affliction; this too in darkness, not light; and again with oft-recurring visitation of His hand.

Next (ver. 4-6) Jeremiah recounts his wearing away; the preparations of Jehovah against him; and his evidently doomed estate. "My flesh and my skin hath he made old; he hath broken my bones. He hath builded against me, and compassed me with gall and travail. He hath set me in dark places, as they that be dead of old," (ver. 4-6).

In verses 7-9, the prophet shows that his portion was not only in imprisonment with heavy chain, but with the awful aggravation that entreaty and prayer could not avail to effect deliverance, the way being fenced, not to protect but to exclude and baffle.

Then Jeremiah draws imagery from the animal kingdom to tell how God spared him in nothing. "He was unto me as a bear lying in wait, and as a lion in secret places. He hath turned aside my ways, and pulled me in pieces: he hath made me desolate. He hath bent his bow, and set me as a mark for the arrow." (ver. 10-12).

Nor does he content himself with telling us how he had been the object of divine attack, as game to the hunter, but lets us see that the mockery of his brethren was not the least part of his trial and bitterness. "He hath caused the arrows of his quiver to enter into my reins. I was a derision to all my people; and their song all the day. He hath filled me with bitterness, he hath made me drunken with wormwood." (ver. 13-15).

Inwardly and outwardly there was every sign of disappointment and humiliation; and expectation of improved circumstances cut off even from Him who is the believer's one resource. "He hath also broken my teeth with gravel stones, he hath covered me with ashes. And thou hast removed my soul far off from peace: I forgat prosperity. And I said, My strength and my hope is perished from Jehovah. (ver. 16-18).

Yet there is the very point of change. From verse 19 he spreads out all before Jehovah, whom he asks to remember it; and from the utter prostration of his soul he begins to conceive confidence. "Remembering mine affliction and my misery, the wormwood and the gall. My soul hath them still in remembrance, and is humbled in me. This I recall to my mind, therefore have I hope." (ver. 19-21). It is not Christ, but assuredly the Spirit of Christ leading on an afflicted and broken heart. Weeping may endure for a night; but joy cometh in the morning.

In what sense then are we to account for language so strong uttered by a holy man, and this not about the persecutions of strangers or the enmity of the Jews, but mostly indeed about Jehovah's ways with him? Certainly not what Calvin and the mass of commentators before and since make of it, as if it were the pressure of the hand of God on the sufferers as Christians when their minds were in a state of confusion and their lips uttered much that is intemperate. Such an interpretation does little honour to God, not to speak of Jeremiah, and makes the Spirit to be a reporter, not merely of a few words or deeds which betray the earthen vessel in its weakness, but of outpourings considerable and minute, which, according to such a view, would consist of scarce anything but complaints spoken according to the judgment of the flesh under feelings so little moderated as to let fall too often things worthy of blame. Can such a view with such results satisfy a thoughtful child of God, who understands the gospel?

I believe, on the contrary, that the language is not hyberbolical, but the genuine utterance of a sensitive

heart in the midst of the crushing calamities of Israel,
or rather now also of Judah and Jerusalem; that they
are the sorrows of one who loved the people
according to God, who suffered with them all the
more because they did not feel as he did that it was
Jehovah Himself who was behind and above their
miseries and shame, inflicting all because of their
sins, with the added and yet keener fact of his own
personal and poignant grief because of what his
prophetic office exposed him to, not so much from
the Chaldeans as from the people of God, his brethren
after the flesh. It was in no way the expression of his
own relation to God as a saint or consequently of
God's feelings towards himself individually; it was
the result of being called of God to take part in Israel
for Him at a time so corrupt and so calamitous. I am
far from meaning that personally Jeremiah did not
know what failure was in that awful crisis. It is plain
from his own prophecy that his timidity did induce
him to sanction or allow on one occasion the deceit of
another, adopting if not inventing it. But he seems to
have been, take him all in all, a rare man, even among
the holy line of the prophets; and, though morbidly
acute in his feelings by nature, singularly sustained of
God with as little sympathy from others as ever fell to
the lot of a servant of God among His people. Even
Elijah's experience fell far short of his, both on the
side of the people's wickedness among whom lay his
ministry, and on the score of suffering inwardly and
outwardly as a prophet who shared all the chastening
which the righteous indignation heaped on his guilty
people, with his own affliction to boot as a rejected
prophet. He appears indeed in this to have the most

nearly approached our blessed Lord, though certainly there was a climax in His case peculiar to Himself, hardly more in the intensely evil and degraded state of Jerusalem then than in he perfection with which He fathomed and felt all before God as one who had deigned to be of them and their chief, their Messiah, who must therefore have so much the deeper interest and the truer sense of what they deserved as a people from God through the instrumentality of their enemies. As a fact this came on them soon after under the last and most terrible siege by Titus; but Jesus went beforehand through all before the cross as well as on it, this apart from making atonement, with which nothing but the densest ignorance could confound it, and mere malice attack others for avoiding its own palpable error.

LAMENTATIONS 3:22-42

THERE is no doubt, I think, that the ground of hope which the prophet lays to heart, as he said in verse 21, is stated in the following verses: "It is of Jehovah's mercies that we are not consumed, because his mercies fail not. They are new every morning: great is thy faithfulness. Jehovah is my portion; therefore will I hope in him." The last clause confirms the thought that verse 21 is anticipative, and that here the spring is touched.

For the turn given by the Targum, and the older versions, save the Vulgate, namely, "The mercies of Jehovah are not consumed, for his compassions fail not," I see no sufficient reason, though Calvin considers this sense more suitable. The Latin and our own version seem to me preferable, not only as being clearer but as giving greater prominence to the persons of His people, and yet maintaining in the last clause what the others spread over both clauses. His mercies then have no end; "they are renewed every morning: great is thy faithfulness. Jehovah is my portion, saith my soul; therefore will I hope in him." It is a goodly portion without doubt, though unbelief thinks it nothing and pines after some one to show any good after a tangible sort, the corn and wine and oil of this creation. But to have Him who has all things and who is Himself infinitely more than all He has is beyond comparison a better portion, as he must own who by grace believes it.

"Jehovah is good to them that wait for him, to the soul that seeketh him. It is good that one should both hope and quietly wait for the salvation of Jehovah. It is good for a man that he bear the yoke in his youth." Confident expectation is thus cherished, while an illusive profession of waiting for Him is detected and judged. For though a careless spirit might pretend to wait for Him, could it be thought of such a one that he is a soul which seeks Him! Activity is implied in this. The next clause asserts the value of patient looking to Him. But it is not tolerable to infer that we err in looking for the continual light of God's favour. For to this redemption entitles us; and Christ is risen the spring and pattern of life in resurrection, on which the Father ever looks with complacency. The last good here contemplated is that one bear the yoke in his youth. Subjection to God's will and to the trials He sends is ever blessed, and this from tender years.

"He sitteth alone and keepeth silence, because he hath borne it upon him. He putteth his mouth in the dust, if so be there may be hope. He giveth his cheek to him that smiteth him: he is filled full with reproach." Thus God's ways are accepted in silence; and humiliation is complete unto death in conscience, yet not without hope; and man's contemptuous persecution and reproach are submitted to.

"For Jehovah will not cast off for ever: but though he cause grief, yet will he have compassion according to the multitude of his mercies. For he doth not afflict willingly nor grieve the children of men." Hope is thus confirmed, without which indeed there is no power of endurance any more than of comfort. His judicial chastenings of Israel are measured and will have an end, as is equally true of His righteous government of ourselves now.

The next triplet is peculiar in its structure, each verse beginning with the infinitive, as is fairly presented in the common Authorized Version. "To crush under his feet all the prisoners of the earth, to turn aside the right of a man before the face of the most high, to subvert a man in his cause, Jehovah approveth not." They are acts of oppression, cruelty, and wrong: should the Lord not see this? Certainly they have no sanction from Him.

The utter ignorance of the future on man's part is next set before us. "Who is he that saith, and it cometh to pass, when Jehovah commandeth it not? Out of the mouth of the most High proceedeth not evil and good? Wherefore doth a living man complain, a man for the punishment of his sins?" All is plainly declared by God. But complainers are never satisfied nor otherwise right. It were better to complain of ourselves, yea every man because of his sins.

Then in verses 40-42 self-judgment is the word of exhortation. "Let us search and try our ways, and turn again to Jehovah. Let us lift up our heart with our hands unto God in the heavens. We have transgressed and have rebelled: thou hast not pardoned." It was just but tremendous thus to find no sign of pardon in His ways.

LAMENTATIONS 3:43-66

NEXT the prophet sets forth without disguise or attenuation the ways of God's displeasure with His people. This was true; and it was right both to feel and to own it, though the owning it to such a God makes it far more painful. "Thou hast covered with anger, and persecuted us; thou hast slain, thou hast not pitied. Thou hast covered thyself with a cloud, that our prayer should not pass through. Thou hast made us as the off scouring and refuse in the midst of the people." (ver. 43-45). There are times when it does not become the saint to seek a deprecation of a chastening—where, if prayer were ignorantly so made, it were a mercy that it should not be heard, And so it was for Jerusalem then. The divine sentence must take its course, however truly God would prove His care of the godly under such sorrowful circumstances.

Then in verses 46-48 he expresses his sense of the reproach heaped on them by their enemies; so that between inward fear and outward desolation the wretchedness was unparalleled. "All our enemies have opened their mouths against us. Fear and a snare is come upon us, desolation and destruction. Mine eye runneth down with rivers of water for the destruction of the daughter of my people." Only those could know it who had been favoured of God as they had been; only one who knew Him as Jeremiah could feel and tell it out as he does. It is but to be expected that some should feel his lamentations to be excessive, as others do the glowing anticipations of the prophets; faith would receive and appreciate both, without criticizing either.

In the next stanza he repeats the words of the last in order to bring Jehovah in. Faith does not hinder but increases grief because of the deplorable state of that which is near to God, when its state is so evil as to be the object of His judgments; yet it is assured that such grief is not unavailing but that He will surely intervene. "Mine eye trickleth down, and ceaseth not, without any intermission, till Jehovah look down, and behold from heaven. Mine eye affecteth mine heart because of all the daughters of my city." (ver. 49-51).

In verses 52-54 the prophet sets forth by various figures the calamities which fall on the Jews from their enemies. "Mine enemies chased me sore, like a bird, without cause. They have cut off my life in the dungeon, and cast a stone upon me. Waters flowed over mine head; then I said, I am cut off." They were no more than as a bird before skilful fowlers, as one shut up in dungeons secured by a stone overhead, as one actually overwhelmed in waters rolling over him.

But prayer may be and has been proved effectual even in their distresses; and so the following verses show as with Jeremiah. "I called upon Thy name, O Jehovah, out of the low dungeon. Thou hast heard my voice: hide not thine ear at my breathing, at my cry. Thou drewest near in the day that I called upon thee; thou saidst, Fear not." (ver. 55-57).

And here it may be as well to point out the danger of those who cite Psalm 22:1, as an ordinary saint's experience, despising or at least failing to use the lesson scripture gives us, that those words suited Jesus on the cross, and certainly no Christian since. He was thus forsaken then that we might never be. It is not then true that the believer under any circumstance is forsaken of God. Jesus only could say in the fulness of the truth, both "My God" and "Why hast thou forsaken me?" And even He never did nor could, I believe, have said these words save as atoning for sin. To suppose that, because David wrote the words, he must have said them as his own experience, is to make the Psalms of private interpretation, instead of recognizing the power of the Spirit who inspired them. Psalm 16 might as well or better be David's experience; yet it needs little discrimination to see that both in their full import belong to Christ exclusively, but in wholly different circumstances.

"O Jehovah, thou hast pleaded the causes of my soul; thou hast redeemed my life. O Jehovah, thou hast seen my wrong; judge thou my cause. Thou hast seen all their vengeance and all their imaginations against me." (ver. 58-60). The prophet is confident that He will appear for vindication and deliverance. The deep and deserved humiliation put on His people does not weaken his assurance or stifle his cry. On the one hand, if He has seen the wrong of the righteous, He would judge his cause; on the other, He had seen all the foe's vengeance and imaginations against him.

This is repeated in the next verses, in connection with what Jehovah had heard. "Thou hast heard their reproach, O Jehovah, and all their imaginations against me: the lips of those that rose up against me, and their device against me all the day. Behold their sitting down, and their rising up; I am their music." (ver. 61-63). At all times throughout their daily life his sorrow was their desired object and liveliest pleasure.

In the closing strain the prophet prays according to the righteous government of God for the earth. "Render unto them a recompense, O Jehovah according to the work of their hands. Give them sorrow of heart, thy curse unto them. Persecute and destroy them in anger from under the heavens of Jehovah." (ver. 64-66). It is no light thing in God's eye that His enemies should find only a matter for mirth in the sufferings and sorrows of those who were under His mighty hand. If the righteous are thus saved with difficulty, what will it be when judgment falls on the ungodly? Even under the gospel we may love and should rejoice in the prospect of the Lord's appearing, though we know what fiery indignation must consume the adversaries. Here of course the prayer is according to a Jewish measure, though none the less just. We are called to higher and heavenly things.

LAMENTATIONS 4:1-11

IT is impossible to view this sorrowful plaint of the prophet as merely historical. Nothing which had ever occurred in the way of disaster or humiliation at all approached the picture of desolation here described. The Spirit of prophecy is therefore forecasting the horrible abyss that awaited the beloved but guilty people.

"How the gold is become dim! the most fine gold is changed! The sacred stones are thrown down at the top of every street! The precious sons of Zion, comparable to fine gold, how they are esteemed as earthen pitchers, the work of the hands of the potter." Who could say that God screened or spared the iniquity of Israel? The most exalted in rank, dignity, and office were those who made their affliction most conspicuous. Could the most obdurate conscience in Jerusalem doubt whose hand had inflicted such reverses, whatever the instrument employed?

Hence the prophet, as he is growingly solemn in his glances at the uttermost distress, so is he calm but the more complete in setting it forth. It is as it were the evil all out, the leper white from head to feet, whose very extremity assures of God's opportunity to interfere both for the Jew and against the adversaries more especially such as ought to pity Jerusalem in the day of her calamity.

That the Chaldean foe should be bitter in reproach and cruel in punishment was not wonderful; but alas! the chosen nation's cup was not full of the indignity they must drink till they were the bitterest, out of sheer want and woe, against their own kin. "Even the dragons [or jackals] draw out the breast, they suckle their young: the daughter of my people [is] cruel like the ostriches in the wilderness." It is of the last bird we read in Job 39:14-17, "which leaveth her eggs in the earth, and warmeth them in the dust, and forgetteth that the foot may crush them, or that the wild beast way break them. She is hardened against her young ones, as though they were not hers: her labour is in vain without fear; because God hath deprived her of wisdom, neither hath he imparted to her understanding."

The sense seems to me certain, though one may not say indisputable, seeing that so sensible a commentator as Calvin contrives to extract a different meaning. He understands the clause to mean that the daughter of the people had come to a savage or cruel one; and hence that whelps of serpents were more kindly dealt with than the Jews. The people had to do with nothing but cruelty, there being no one to succour them in their miseries. Thus the force would be, not that the people are accused of cruelty in not nourishing their children, but that they were given up to the most relentless of enemies. But I see no force in his reasoning which appears to be founded on unacquaintance with the Hebrew idiom, the masculine gender being used for emphasis where formally we might have expected the feminine, as not infrequently happens. Hence there is no real ground for going on with the allusion to the ostrich, as if the prophet meant that the Jews were so destitute of every help that they were banished into solitary places beyond the sight of men.

The true meaning is far more expressive and sets forth the awful state of the Jews, when not enemies only but those who should have been their own tenderest protectors were destitute of feelings found in the fiercest brutes, and only comparable for heartlessness to creatures of the most exceptional hardness and folly. Such were the mothers of Salem in the outpouring of Jeremiah's grief.

Accordingly in verse 4 he pursues the case. "The tongue of the suckling cleaveth to its palate for thirst; infants ask bread—none breaketh [it] for them." Such was the pitiable state of children from the tenderest days upward. Was it any better with their elders? "They that fed daintily perish in the streets; they who were brought up on scarlet embrace dung hills." (ver. 5). Parents and other adults were famishing and dying of hunger, and this gladly as it were on the dunghill instead of the splendid couches on which they used to recline when weary of pleasure itself.

Next the prophet draws out the proof that the vengeance under which the people were was worse than that of Sodom, especially in this, that the notorious city of the plain was overwhelmed in a sudden blow of destruction, whereas that of Jerusalem was prolonged and most varied agony. "For the punishment of the iniquity of the daughter of my people is greater than the punishment of the sin of Sodom, that was overthrown as in a moment, and no hands stayed on her." (verse 6). The "hands" of man

added to the soreness of the Jewish chastening:
Sodom was dealt with by God without any human
intervention. Compare the feeling of David when he
brought to the verge of ruin the people whom God
had entrusted him to feed. (2 Sam. 24:13,14).

Nor does any consecration to God avail to shelter:
so complete the ruin, so unsparing the vengeance let
loose on every class and every soul. "Her Nazarites
were brighter than snow, they were whiter than milk;
they were more ruddy in body than rubies (or coral),
their cutting (shape) of sapphire. Their aspect is
darker than dusk, they are not known in the streets;
their skin cleaveth to their bones, it is dried up like a
stick." Nothing availed in presence of these searching
desolating judgments. The blessing which was once
so marked on those separated was now utterly and
manifestly fled, yea, wretchedness as under His ban
had taken its place. And so truly was it so, that he
proceeds to show how but a choice of ills awaited the
Jew, a violent death or a life yet more horrible.
"Happier the slain with the sword than the slain with
hunger; because these pine away pierced through for
the fruits of the field," i.e., for the want of them. For
it is very forced to take it as Calvin does, pierced
through by the fruits of the earth, as if the productions
of the earth became swords.

So obliterated were all traces of compassion or
even natural feeling that, as we are next told, "the
hands of pitiful women boiled their children; they
became their food in the destruction of the daughter
of my people." (ver. 10). Nothing could account for
such barbarity but that which he adds immediately
after (ver. 11): "Jehovah hath spent his fury; be hath

poured out his fierce anger, and hath kindled a fire in Zion which hath devoured her foundations." What can be more thorough than to devour foundations? So it was declared of God against Jerusalem for their heinous sins. Impossible to escape His hand stretched out against His own: how deep their sin and vain to deny it!

LAMENTATIONS 4:12-22

VERSE 12 introduces a new topic, which gives remarkable vividness to the prophet's picture of Jerusalem's desolation. It was not the king of Judah who was surprised at the taking of his capital, but the kings of the earth who treated it as incredible that they could force it; it was not the Jews merely who fondly dreamt that their city was impregnable, but all the inhabitants of the world gave up the hope as vain. "The kings of the earth, and all the inhabitants of the world, would not have believed that the adversary and the enemy should have entered into the gates of Jerusalem." (ver. 12).

This prepares the way for a fresh exposure of the real causes of Jerusalem's ruin. Their sins were so glaring, where they were most odious and offensive, that God must have denied Himself if He had not brought His people down to the dust and scattered them to the ends of the earth. "Because of the sins of her prophets, the iniquities of her priests that have shed the blood of the just in the midst of her, they wandered blind in the streets, they were defiled with blood, so that men could not touch their garments." (ver. 13, 11). The greater the privilege in having such servants of Jehovah, the more distressing that they should pollute His name and people.

There is no reason that I know for Calvin's version of the last clause of verse 14: "They were defiled with blood, because they could not but touch their garments." It seems indeed an ungrounded departure from the common and correct translation, both in giving the reason where it should be rather a statement of consequence, and in needlessly supposing a particle which brings in a very different idea. Nor do I see any just meaning in what results; for where would be the force of saying that they were defiled with blood because they could not but touch their garments? One could understand pollution from such contact, but hardly with blood from it. As the clause stands in the common version, the import appears to be that wandering blindly in the streets they defiled themselves in the worst way possible, with blood, so that their very garments must pollute any who might touch them. So universal was the defilement of the holy city that the clothes of the inhabitants could not be touched without contamination to others. There was as it were a fretting leprosy in the whole body politic. "Depart, unclean, they called out to them; depart, depart, touch not. So they flee away and also wander. They say among the nations, they shall dwell no more [there]." Thus most graphically does the prophet show that the exile of the Jew from the land was inevitable and of another character from an ordinary deportation of a people through the cruelty of a conqueror or the jealousy of an ambitious rival nation. It was in vain for the Jews to flatter themselves that it was God employing them for a season as a missionary people: God will send them forth; a few preparatorily to the kingdom, and when it is set up yet more largely as a nation. But here it is a people once holy, now profane, not honoured in a gracious service and a grave trust, but punished for their dishonour of His law and sanctuary, and hence outcasts so ignominious that they flee themselves like lepers, proclaiming their own defilement and misery. So complete is the ruin that among the nations it is said, They shall no more sojourn in their land and city.

But this is an error. Impossible that God should be defeated by Satan, good by evil, in the long run. Appearances in this world ever give such expectations; and unbelieving man is as ready to credit them as to doubt God. But in the midst of judgment God remembers mercy; and therefore the more unsparing He might be, the more assuredly He would turn again with deliverance for His own name's sake. "The face [i.e. anger] of Jehovah hath divided them, he will no more regard them: they respected not the faces of the priests, they spared not the elders." (ver. 16). Undoubtedly their overthrow was complete, and the contempt of the enemy so much the better because their success was beyond their own hopes; for there had ever been a lurking fear that God would avenge their wrongs and once more espouse the cause of His people. But now that He gave them up to the will of His adversaries, their pleasure was to wound them to the quick in the persons of the most honoured sons of Zion.

And what could the prophet say in extenuation? He could only add here another heavy fault: "As yet for us [i.e., while we yet remained], our eyes failed for our vain help; on our watchtowers we watched for a nation that could not save us." (ver. 17). They turned with longing desires after Egypt against the

Chaldeans, instead of turning to God in repentance of heart, spite of reiterated warning from His prophets not to trust in an arm of flesh, least of all in that broken reed.

But no: sentence was passed by God, incensed with the unwearied evils of His people; and the fiercest of the heathen were let loose as executors of His wrath upon them. "They hunted our steps, so that we could not walk in our streets; our end was near, our days were fulfilled, for our end had come. Our persecutors are swifter than the eagles of the heaven: they pursued us upon the mountains, they laid wait for us in the wilderness." (ver. 18, 19). No mountain was steep, no desert lonely, enough to protect the guilty fugitives. It was God who was punishing them by means most just, yet to them most painful, for their revolt from Himself.

Alas! the remnant returned from Babylon have only added another and incomparably worse sin in the rejection of the Messiah and the refusal of the gospel, so that wrath is come upon them to the uttermost.

But even then how lamentable the desolation! "The breath of our nostrils, the anointed of Jehovah, was taken in their pits, of whom was said, Under his shadow we shall live among the heathen." (ver. 20). It is of course Zedekiah who is alluded to. They had hoped in his office, whatever his demerits personally, forgetting that all the honour God bestowed on it was in view of Christ, who alone shall bear the glory. But their hearts were in the present, not really for Messiah; and they had only to lie down disappointed in sorrow.

Did Edom then taunt their fallen brother in the day of his distress? Indeed they did it with murderous treacherous hatred too. Hence the apostrophe of the prophet. "Rejoice and be glad, O daughter of Edom, that dwellest in the land of Uz; the cup also shall pass through unto thee: thou shalt be drunken, and shalt make thyself naked. The punishment of thine iniquity is accomplished, O daughter of Zion; he will no more carry thee away into captivity: he will visit thine iniquity, O daughter of Edom; he will discover thy sins." (ver. 21, 22). Did they say in the day of Jerusalem, Down with it, down with it to the very foundation? They too must be brought to shame. If the Chaldean swept the holy land, the daughter of Edom must await no less when her day came to be carried away captive for her sins.

LAMENTATIONS 5

THE last chapter differs from all before in that the
alphabetic series drops, though there are
evidently twenty-two verses as in other cases, with
the modification we have seen in chapter 3 and its
triplets. Internally also the elegy approaches more to
the character of a prayer as well as a compressed
summing up of the sorrows detailed before.

Hence, says the prophet, "Remember, O Jehovah,
what hath happened to us; behold, and look on our
reproach. Our inheritance is turned over to strangers,
our houses to aliens." (ver. 1, 2). It was not merely
a human or natural feeling of their loss and
degradation. We must bear in mind that Israel had the
land of their possession from Jehovah. No doubt they
expelled or subjugated the Canaanites. According to
men they held by right of conquest. But a deeper fact
lay underneath the successes of Joshua. Strength was
given from God to put down the most corrupt race
then on the face of the earth who had intruded into a
land which He had from the first destined and given
by promise to the fathers. For when the most High
divided to the nations their inheritance, when He
separated the sons of man, He set the bounds of the
tribes according to the number of the sons of Israel.
Alas! they took the blessing not as promises by faith
on the ground of God's grace, but under the condition
of their own fidelity to the law—a condition

necessarily fatal to the sinner. Hence the disasters, and finally ruin, which Jeremiah here groans out to God. But the title, in which Moses (Deut. 32:8) had thus declared His purpose as to His people, is to be noted; for it is His millennial name more specially than any other, and hence that by which Melchizedek is characterized, who typifies the day of blessing after the victory is won over the assailing and previously triumphant kings of the Gentiles. Thus there is assured hope in the end for the scattered and peeled people of God. Meanwhile how bitter the sight of their inheritance transferred to the foreigners, their houses to strangers!

"We are orphans and without a father, our mothers [are] as widows." (ver. 3). Even this did not convey a vivid enough picture of their desolation. The common possession of all, the freest uses of their land, belonged to hard masters. "Our water have we drunk for money; our wood cometh for a price. On our necks [i.e. with a yoke on them] are we persecuted; we toil and have no rest." (ver. 4, 5). What slaves so abject? And this Jeremiah who did not go to Babylon stayed long enough to see, and feel, and spread in sorrow before God. "To Egypt we gave the hand and to Asshur to be satisfied with bread." (ver. 6). But neither could effectually help, still less could either resist the king of Babylon; and this because of Israel's sins which had so long called for an avenger. "Our fathers sinned [and are] not; and we bear their iniquities." (ver. 7). This, we know, was become a proverbial complaint about this time. (Ezek. 18). But God tried them on their own ground, with precisely the same result of ruin because of their evil. For if fathers and children are alike sinful, the punishment is due whether for those or for these: come it must if God judges. How much better then to repent than to repine and murmur, only aggravating the evil and ensuring vengeance on such accumulating rebellion against God!

"Slaves rule over us: no one delivereth us out of their hand. With our lives[1] we bring in our bread because of the sword of the wilderness. Our skins[1] glow like an oven because of the hot blasts of famine. Women have they ravished in Zion, virgins in the cities of Judah. Princes were hung up by their hand; the faces of elders they honoured not. Young men they took to the mill, and boys fell under the wood. Aged men have ceased from the gate, young men from their song. The joy of our heart hath ceased; our dance is turned into mourning. The crown of our head is fallen: woe now unto us, for we have sinned! Because of this our heart is faint; for these our eyes are dim; because of the mount of Zion which is desolate, foxes walk about on it." (ver. 8-18). Such is the dismal state so pathetically described by a heart crushed under grief which could not exaggerate the prostration of God's ancient people. Sex, age, condition, place—nothing spared, and nothing sacred. Every word carries weight, not a particular which is not an intolerable burden. How overwhelming for the heart which justly feels everything!

Thus mournfully had Jeremiah's warnings been executed. As Shiloh had been profaned, so now the

---

[1] The plural is given by many excellent MSS.; probably softened into the singular by the rest.

place of Jehovah's choice, the mount Zion that he loved. The outward indefectibility of His dwelling on earth is but the fond dream of the men whose unrighteousness, holding the truth in unrighteousness, will surely bring on its judgment from the enemy under the righteous dealing of God.

What then is the resource of the faithful? Never the perpetuity of what is visible, never the first man, but the Second. "Thou, O Jehovah, remainest for ever; thy throne from generation to generation" (ver. 19). Hence the righteous cry with the assurance that His ears are open, even though He tarry and justly rebuke sin especially in those that bear His name, in whom He will be sanctified by His judgments till they by grace sanctify Him in their hearts.

God however will have His blows felt; and faith does feel and gather blessing even in the grief, while it looks onward to the day. The foolish pass on and are punished, harden themselves and perish in unbelief. "Wherefore dost thou forget us for ever?— forsake us for a length of days?" (ver. 20). But there is no despair, though the way was then dark before the true light shone; for the heart pleads, "Turn thou us unto thee, O Jehovah, and we shall be turned; renew our days as of old. For certainly thou hast utterly rejected us, thou hast been exceedingly wroth with us." (ver. 21, 22). To own our own sins and God's judgment is the constant effect of the Spirit's work in the heart, the sure pledge of coming and better blessing in store for us from the God of all grace.